Roland Sez, etc.

# Roland Sez, etc.

Poems by Roland Pease

Zoland Editions

Published by Zoland Editions
Cambridge, Massachusetts
zolandeditions@gmail.com

ISBN: 979-8-218-05145-7

Copyright © 2022 by Roland Pease

Other books by Roland Pease:
*Inside Out* (Zoland Editions)
*Variety Store* (Zoland Editions)

Book design by Peter Paul Payack
www.pppayack.com

My poems are alphabetized, because it works for me and I hope it works for you. This collection may seem like a grab bag of sorts, but each poem has been carefully selected to add up to a self-portrait of a kind. Some of the poems are older, some new, and some are in-between, adding up to a likeness of me. Welcome aboard.

*Dedicated to all (cool) cats,
past, present and future*

"Whoever is in a hurry will not stop for me."

– Camille Pissarro

Roland Sez, etc.

**A Captive Audience**

Listening to poultry.
Bound and gagged,
and lulled beyond
measure, their ears
wiggled to be free
from poetry; easier
said than done. The
reader paused, then
gurgled and waited
again significantly.
A silence sounded
divine like wine you
spill in dreams. I was
thinking about the Red Sox.
Language, or the very lick of it,
ruled, punctuating that evening.
Half the audience was sunk and
as restless as could be. When all
was said and done, done and then
some, gags were removed—writer's rags--
and we moved on. The happening happened.
Was this one nightmare gone round the bend?
The happy listeners stayed seated, their great
expectations had been more than met, deep in
the minds of a few who could not forget, could
not remember what they were thinking, and why. So
applause wasn't called for in the least, no, not. Their
noggins were nodding such approval; bobbing heads.

## Aghast

The law of the
land sucks the
big one much
of the time. I
have been on
the sidelines
sometimes; I
have been in
the thick of it
other times.
That's beside
the point. The
point is it's so
hard to locate
justice now-a-
days. I am left
aghast too often.
All's out of hand,
I'm sorry to say.
So begin at once
to change things.
Work from dawn
to dawn, or else.
No time to waste.
Never say: not me.
Perish the thought.
Black Lives Matter.
You surely know it.
Change your ways
before it gets later
than you think it is.

**Bunt**

When you don't
know what else

to do lay one
down. Catch

them off guard
playing footsie.

They won't like
you one bit, but

who the hell cares.
Get on base. Put the

pressure on-- then
use your speed and

steal a base or two.
Your name isn't Slow

Mo for nothing. All
those in favor say aye.

A sight to be seen.
Don't mess around,

get a grip, then we'll
see what we will see.

Slide with spikes up high.
Break the rules once more.

Winning is the only game in
town, don't you just know it.

**Cattle Crossing #7**

In such funny company.
Bovines. Got to love 'em.

Running across the field
with them in hot pursuit.

Cracks me up when
I think about it now.

The Road Runner
had nothing on me.

A bad case of the spooks.
Cow legs coming after me.

Those gigantic heads bouncing
about, pointing in my direction.

Dozens and dozens of sharp
horns aiming at me. Oh boy.

A laugh and a half. Moo.
They scared me to death

when they all decided
to take off after me. No

joke. A trying time.
There was such hell

to pay, wipe that
fear off your face,

farmer-boy. It puts
hair on your chest.

Leaping over that fence
at the very last moment.

**Clever Devil**

My mind's eye is full of tricks.
No woolgathering going on in
there. No Drowsy Time Club. I

plea for sleep from time to time,
and dreams are delighted to take
over. Some need to bank my bets.

Thoughts pick up steam even if
I say slow down. My mind has a
mind of its own I venture to say.

**Epitome**

It is her name,
believe it or not.

Keep an eye
out for her.

In this day & age
everything goes.

My name is Jitter-
bug, what's yours?

If nothing else, she is an
example of a modern soul

and that is justification
enough. Well done for her.

The modern age is here. Again.
It comes around & goes around.

Epitome, indeed. Join the crowd.
We're the new. We are the proud.

**Found Poem**

*Court Sentences Cat to the Indoors for Life*
(1983 Passau, West Germany)

Thousands of West German animal lovers,
outraged by a court ruling on Bubu,
a two-year-old black and gray alley cat,
are flooding this town with letters and telegrams of solidarity.

The uproar stems from a ruling "sentencing" Bubu
to life imprisonment. Bubu's owners are ordered
to keep their cat, "inside forever" or they will be
fined about $190,000.00 if Bubu is found again
prowling through a neighbor's garden. The neighbor,
who doesn't even live next door, complained of Bubu's
frequent visits. Since the ruling, the post office has been
swamped with letters, some simply addressed to "Cat Bubu,
Passau, currently in detention." A cat demonstration had been
recommended from, "cat Willy."

Another cat lover expressed the wish that the neighbor
responsible for Bubu's plight would have, "multitudes" of rats
invade his home.

## Hanging Out

Becoming conscious
of the heights: a view

of what nods hello,
magical--situation

near Harvard Square
once again. One with

an ally-- will be, must be.
Serenity. Supposing. Fun

together with someone who
knows what to say, then do.

The long and the short of it suits us
fine. Wind up the toys for the kiddos,

and break out the words, guzzling beliefs until
you can't any longer. Befriend the Dalmatians.

**Just Passing By**

The big fellow was schlepping
in the other direction when I
heard him say, "I think I'm
going to have a cow." He
seemed very upset, I felt
badly for him, and so
I asked him what he
really meant by that.
"Oh," he said, "that's just
an old expression. I'm not
having a superb day. Thanks
for asking." I watched him walk
away, slowly, sadly. I wanted to
go after him, but to do what? I left
well enough alone, yet my mood was
less than good for the next minutes or more.
I tried out the expression I had heard, about
having a cow, and I too was misunderstood.
Sometimes language fails to do the job well
enough, yet it is all we have at our disposal.

**Let the Moment Pass**

Weather systems indicate
that we are in for tougher

times ahead. Buckle up.
Are you in the swing of

things-- up to speed in
general? Stealth attacks

are forecast. Peter says
so, and he should know.

I cannot speak to that. I
just saw lightning like I've

never seen it before. These
electrical storms are nothing

like I have ever witnessed. It
must have to do with climate

change, the dumb nuts who never
could listen to others in the know.

Let the moments pass only if you must
believe they're merely inconsequential.

**Mad Dash**

And what a one it was.
Merriment was a part

of it, for sure. Figures
were romping around.

Impossible not to enjoy
the antics. This was all

brought about by nice
news. What a day lay

there before us. Glee
like that doesn't come

by all that often. We'd never
be quite the same. I heard

some singing: "Happy
Days Are Here Again."

What do you want?
Steady diet of this!

Stand-up guys & gals
took their clothes off.

Wreaking havoc, ahoy.
Sending shock waves.

An adventure had
started. Hats off!

## My Union Card

Stumbled across it just now
in a pile of crap I keep. I was

a member of the AFL-CIO for
a short period of time. Roland

E. Peace was my name, according
to them, in 1/69, back when I was

with the A.P., a wire-photo operator
in the day before fax machines. Took

in many photos from the moon, from Woodstock, N.Y.,
Manson etc... I worked in their darkroom doing their

jobs, and my own, into the early hours of the
a.m. Quit there to attend photography school,

and to where I sit at the present moment. I am a
loyal union person through & through, are you?

**Not Hardly**

> "Everyone has a place in history.
> Mine is clouds." – Richard Brautigan

In it for the long haul,
however long or short

that can be, follow me.
The way of the world is

all about the whys and
the wherefores, isn't it?

Scruples are necessary,
or is it rubles, one or the

other, or maybe both. I,
for one, am kind of clue-

less on this subject, or
maybe that's what I'm

saying to put you off the
track. Got to scram now.

## Not Shakespeare

Never said I was.
Good news, bad

news: nobody
will ever take

the time to
memorize

my words,
of that I'm

absolutely
certain. So

be it. I go with
that knowledge.

Maybe Poem/Poe
is the exception.

Accept it as Fate.
Am one with it. A-

OK. It is what it is.
Sizable shoes to fill.

I am after it every day.
Too big for my britches

only on rare occasions,
I am the one and only

one I need to answer to.
I put my specs on daily.

## Novel #3

A shaky truce had us eating out of both sides of our mouths, talking that way too, not knowing exactly what the heck-hell was going on, to be honest about it. Neither of us went to Harvard, neither of us had any jitters in the mornings, either. We did get antsy from time to time, and visited the saloon on the corner for solace and salsa, not to mention the best beans this side of wherever. Our good friends were horses, mine was tan, his was white, and we knew how to gallop like sons of bitches. The day came when we were way too old to saddle up, and we still got along famously, rocking in our rockers, telling the tallest tales we could tell. Nobody listened to us.

**Photographs**

Shot them.
Developed
them, too.
Black and
white. Not

shots of cereal.
None of models.
Politics, yes, and
patterns: abstract.
Lyrical. At a certain

point, I moved away from
chemicals and technology,
returning to my pen, to the
page, discovering poems more
to my liking, notions that were

informed by the photographs
I took when I was developing
a writer's eye, such as it was, is…
There has always been something
I wanted to say one way or another.

**Play Ball**

Spring training
is finally here.

All those Pros
and Prospects

coming at you
for fun & profit.

Slug that long-ball,
steal a base or two,

just for me and my
buddies. We'll cheer,

holler, but boo you, too.
Take it to the next level.

We do know the difference.
We are here to urge you on.

It is a young man's sport,
but as a fan you can age.

Win or lose, warmer weather is
making a comeback in our yard.

I'll get juvenile again and root for
my team to rough up your team.

Year after year this beat goes on.
We are aging fast. We move along.

**Please Listen to Me**

I have something
to state to you; do
read on if you will.

I am a writer with
much on my mind.
Proceed if you can.

Up in the night, I
write, "I will pave
the way if you let

me. I won't give
you a hard time.
I am your friend."

I can't push it off,
these words, what
I want to say right

now. My cat is my
companion who is
by my side, always.

I live with my dear
wife, as well, and
our cat's our chum,

the one in the middle
of the night, sitting by
me in a manuscript box

next to my desk as I write.
She will never know what I
have to say, but she's willing

to keep me company. I worship
her for her being, for her quiet.
We have our moments together.

**Red Cap**

I did it for a year.
Not a bad way to
make one's wages.

Got great tips,
and bad ones,
and none at all.

Wasted no time
doing what
needed doing.

From day to day
in every way, I
pushed my luck.

I'm a professional
in whatever form
it ends up taking.

I had to carry a
heavy container
with a python in-

side. Creeped me
out... One young
lovely kissed me

hard on the mouth.
As good as it gets.
I should have quit

when I was ahead.
Got punched by a
drunk who thought

I was his long-lost
brother—I went on
to be a big shot box-

er--my life is odd
enough to interest
me in a weird way.

**Roland Sez #44**

Safe and sound.
So it is tonight.

Flames in the fire-
place. A good book

to keep me going for
awhile. My wife and

children are nearby in
terrific moods. Grieg's

playing in the back-
ground. A storm has

gone by, and dinner is
being digested. In the

back of my mind I know
this too will pass, but I

am wise enough to take
it in. Relish it. Read on.

If I cannot rest easy now, then
I'm failing the biggest test of all.

## Roland Sez #50

Looks like a horse race.
Down to the wire: we're

going to get there by gum.
The real rewards are un-

certain, but I've always
enjoyed the unknown.

Much of it to delight in.
We are close, but then

so are the Joneses, nip and
tuck, barreling for the edge

of the finish line. Destiny
is wearing a smirk, about

to crown one of us the lucky
duck. Second place receives

nothing, a mad journey home.
Such is the way of our world.

## Roland Sez #95

My life is passing
before my very
eyes; I must
head for the
hills, but I
heard
there's
a traffic
snarl-up
up there.
Road rage
is rampant.
Wall to wall
consternation.
One parking lot
of people on the
race to elsewhere.
Bless us as we depart
for the greener pastures.
What choice do we have?
I'm convinced I am going
to exist forever in one form
or another. I can't prove it,
certainly, but you can't tell
me we end up in the trash.
That goes against all reason,
with such storylines started,
with the complexities within.

## Roland Sez #239

> "Men should stop fighting among
> themselves and start fighting insects."
> – Luther Burbank, Horticulturist

Bugs. Everywhere
you look you view
them coming near.

Millions of them.
Perhaps billions.
Wear your spray.

Look sharp and
carry a swatter.
Swear like hell.

No worries, you
state, but who
the hell knows.

They could take
over. There's a first
time for everything.

If you don't watch
out, you'll sure be
wishing you had.

## Roland Sez #240

How's tricks?
He always
says that
to himself
as he goes
about his
business.
Amuses
himself
no end.
Why not?
Priceless.
Love fest.
Live wire.
Class act.
Merely one
of those things.
Pegged as such.
Getting through
the day once again.
Funny that, habits.
Speaking his piece.
There's our business
here on planet Earth.
Reading things into it.
This point of no return.

## Roland Sez #242

Heavens to Mergatroyd.
I go a long-ways back.
The things I know &

  you never will can fill
  an attic or three. You
  call me a geezer and I

    wear the title with pride.
    Why not? Might as well.
    Not getting any younger.

## Roland Sez #255

That is all there is to it,
and you know it as well
as I do. Now we are cooking.
An A-ha moment is not even
close to occurring anytime soon.
Birdy down the street was kicking
up dust, and the neighbors were
not a bit thrilled by it, either.
But screw them and their
idle ways. That is what I
have to say at this moment.
I'm out-of-sorts, having foot
cramps like you wouldn't be-
lieve, biding my time, keeping
my eyes as open as open can be.

## Roland Sez #257

Thunk. A noise in the night.
A know-it-all once informed
me that unexplained clamor
has to do with ghosts, their
need to make themselves a
space in our lives. He was
a dipshit, but I have never
forgotten his words. Once
I saw his mug-shot in the
Post Office, wanted for being
nothing less than a thug and
a scoundrel, someone to take
notice of, take seriously. That
took me aback. Knocks in the
night; things he knows about.

# Roland Sez #263

> "With me poetry has not been
> a purpose, but a passion."
> – Edgar Allan Poe

Don't be a stranger.
She said that to me.

Always strangers,
all the time, we're

left without a pot
to piss in, if you

will, most of the time,
metaphorically speak-

ing, you understand.
Please bear with me.

We've got places to go,
and people to see, and

so we don't know what
is occurring. Do poems

interest you? Because
they'll slow you down:

read them, write them;
try that going forward.

Do focus on your breathing.
The rest is merely weather.

**Roland Sez #266**

Catch me if you can.
I've got a head's start,
but you claim to be a
whiz at locating run-
aways so here goes. I

was so looking forward
to this delightful game
of deceit and patience.
I've circled around and
am now in the kitchen

drinking a Budweiser.
You are undoubtedly
still in the fields, full
of annoyance at those
nettles that have had a

way with you. My beer
is tasty and I think I'll
dip into a bag of chips.
Soon you'll double back
and find me, and that is

precisely what I am hoping for.
There should still be two hours
for us to enjoy a lovely time of it.
Sometimes your challenges can be
trying, but I frequently find 'em fun.

## Roland Sez #279

Feckless is a funny word,
vainglorious as well. It's
your assignment, if you
choose to take it on, to
use both words in the
same sentence later
on today. I tell you
it can be done. If
you don't get a
look or two I'd
be surprised.
Impromptu.
Keep them
guessing.
Now go
and do,
pronto.

## Roland Sez #325

> "Bye bye love, bye bye sweet caress, hello
> emptiness, I feel like I could di-ie."

The Everly Brothers.
The first rock album
I ever bought. Those
late nineteen fifties.

Couldn't get enough
of it. Rev me up why
don't you, count me
in, call me zany now.

Getting on in years.
Aging begrudgingly.
Letting bygones be
bygones. Why not?

My street cred does
not exist anymore.
Rock' n roll glory days
are long gone. Museums

are my speed nowadays,
and I am fine with that.
Arp has my number.
Dove does as well.

## Roland Sez #336

> "Every tooth in a man's head is more
> valuable than a diamond." – Cervantes

A dentist after
my own heart.

"Here's the rub,"
he once uttered.

That doc hums
as he works. As

long as he does
not twiddle his

thumbs. Sees
cavities now

and again, is
known to say,

"Beats me,"
from time

to time. I
have no

idea what
he's talk-

ing about.
My mouth

is wide open,
stuffed with

cotton and
utensils. A

nice enough
guy, a sailor.

Uttering &
muttering.

## Roland Sez $376

Not to be trusted,
not by a long shot.

We had words, and
then our words had

words. Helluva day.
It grabs me so when

we don't see eye to eye.
Eyesore Arguments. If

you were aboveboard it
would be one thing, but

you aren't. A schemer. I,
by and large, am better

than that, although not all
the time. Humans together.

In no time flat, we are at it
again, kicking our can down

the road some more, making
amends, building that bridge

to nowhere, fast, gathering
thoughts together as we do.

**Roland Sez #384**

Summer is
here again.
Bless it so.

Birds
sound
in our

ears.
Mine.
Yours.

Having fun
with you
in Vermont.

Less clothing.
Long evenings.
Great rewards.

Reading, writing,
and thinking
more than ever.

The Winter was
a poke in the eye.
Not hardly easy.

It was quite telling.
Too long and hard.
One way or another.

Time slowed
to a crawl
as snow fell.

Baseball is now
at Fenway Park.
This is our year.

Just being now
one more time
is enough for me.

## Roland Says #435

Share and share
alike has often
been my motto,
but that can be
asking for trouble.
Just see my friend,
Hank. He got into
a heap of concern
the other day. He
loaned out his car.
Boom, bam, damn.
Hold your tongue.
Sure, if you say so.
I shudder to think.
You know the drill.

**Roland Sez #436**

Ups and downs.
Recoil. Totter. I
shirk my duties
only on occasion.

The going concern
today has to do with
mind-blowing head-
lines. What do we do?

I am good for my word,
and if I say I'll do some-
thing, I will, so hear me
out. I'll be here for you.

Dial it up, dial it back,
do whatever it takes.
I'm in over my head.
So what else is new?

Will we go to war?
Will we impeach
him? Will we,
will we not?

## Roland Sez #440

Sorry about that. Lip service. Shown the door. In a huff, sealing a deal, I must gather my thoughts before much more time goes on. I've said my two cents, now I must devise a plan, or people will believe I don't know my bass from my trout. I've had the gall to be outspoken; now deliver the goods. If I am to be taken seriously, by myself and others, I will have to elevate my game. Here is doing my all.

## Roland Sez #441

Drop everything.
Coming together.
Our planet needs
us to gather our
strength and make
a good go of it. The
riddles in the room
are stomping about
big time. I'd say let's go
separate ways, but that
is no longer a possibility.
We're in this thing together.
There's a chain of command,
you know it, and I know it all
too well, but who they are, and
where they are, is so debatable.

# Roland Sez #503

Writing in this blizzard,
indoors, alone, have my
book to write; God help
me in my time of musing.

One word follows another,
like that, years' worth, and
what will it amount to, what
will its value be? You tell me.

An up-to-the-moment report.
It is common knowledge that
I'm wrestling this Beast with
all I've got deep inside of me.

I have my thinking cap on most
of the time, even when I dream.
I fight the good fight, and though
I may not win, I don't plan to lose.

## Roland Sez #531

I'm keeping a running tally.
That is one of my talents. I
have notes all over, keeping
tabs on things. Yes, why not.
It might come in handy, you
never know: when I did that,
when I heard you humming,
when something crossed my
mind. What's with that, some
of my friends say. What's with
you, I state right back at them.
I saw seven runaway horses, and
wrote it down, because you never
know, do you. One escaped mental
moment. Two jolly dogs. It adds up.
Tallying things up runs in the family.
The long & short of it is multifaceted.

## Roland Sez #547

I am standing guard
so wounded in woe.
Frozen stiff, as well.
It has been a helluva
night in the neighbor-
hood. Much hangs in
the balance, per usual.
I turn up the loud music.
Ellington slays me again.
Our cat has gone missing.

**Salt Lake City**
**(of all places)**

Drifting into town on my way across the country,
I was delirious, foggy-brained, and needed a real
rest, or at least one hotel room without fleas. Got

one, six floors up. So where the holy hell was I,
I wondered: more or less on my way elsewhere.
People were pleasant. The sun looked the same.

Food had a metallic taste, but that could've been
my oddball taste buds, my own burden. I was in
line at the supermarket--needing beer and bread--

and heard a reunion taking place behind me. Squeals
of delight. "What are you doing these days?" "Un-
employed." "Oh." "Are you in the book? I'm in the

book. Let's call and get together one of these days." I
realized I was not in the book, theirs, or any other, drift-
ing from one location to another, avoiding all reunions.

I was starved for bread, beer, a tub, T.V., and a bed before
heading out the next day for some other destination... My
youth. Vagabond. The 1970s. Bound for much better days.

**Saving Face**

> "I have never made but one
> prayer to God, a very short
> one: 'O Lord, make my
> enemies ridiculous.' And
> God granted it." – Voltaire

Save Lives Not Face.
My bumper sticker
states much, gets
annoyed looks,
quite the point.

Baffled motorists
scratch their heads,
maybe think some,
maybe they should.
War is a lousy state

to have to move through,
and it must be eradicated.
Committing aggression is
out of the question. I need
to move to another part of

the universe, into a community
that comprehends compassion.
That notion seems to have flown
the coop, with manners & decency.
I only pray on a bad day, but know

what the power of caring can do. Dumb
people rule this thorny world nowadays.
Couldn't we do better by flipping a coin?
Small minds articulate lies so much quicker,
then they wangle their ways to the top. Time

for a swim, I believe-- off to the water I must go. Let your
little leaders drown in their own guilt and deep deceptions.
Somewhere, somehow, they'll meet their maker, and I know
they will be forced to witness endless reruns of their sins. But
then they'll most likely chortle, enjoying their own reflections.

**Session #1**

On the cusp,
I boiled over.

Damn straight.
Blotto. Groggy.

Spellbound for sure.
Daydreams mix it up.

I will salvage what
I have, no problem.

But of course, I am a nut,
that goes without saying,

and I'm smack dab in the middle
of the wildest voodoo party ever.

**Sleeping Like a Log**

Be gone with you.
Lights out. Sweet
dreams. Tone it
down. Recharge.
What are you do-
ing there in your
depths? Making
red poems out of
overturned apple
carts just like me?

**Sounds Seen and Heard**

A Living Poem (last updated January 2026)

Abdullah Ibrahim, Adventure Set, Aimee Mann and 'Till Tuesday, Al Cohn, Al Kooper, Alan Dawson (2), Alan Vega, Alberta Hunter, Alex Degrassi, Alicia de Larrocha, Amir ElSaffar and the Two Rivers Ensemble, Anat Cohen Quartetinho, Andre Watts, Angelique Kidjo, Ani DiFranco, Anna Unchu Pyon, Annie Fischer, Anton Heiller, Arlo Guthrie, Arturo Sandival, Avishai Cohen, B52s, Bad Acid Trip, Ball and Pivot, Band 19, Barbara Higbie, BB King (2), Beausoleil (2), Bernadette Peters, Bette Carter, Big Country, Billy Bragg, Billy Squiers, Blues Heritage Orchestra, Bob Dylan (3), Bobby Rydell, Bobby Timmons, Brandenberg Ensemble, Bruce Katz, Bruce Springsteen (2), Bruce Woolly and The Camera Club, Buckwheat Zydeco, C.J. Chenier (2) and his Red Hot Louisiana Band, Canned Heat, Cannonball and Nat Adderly (2), Carole King, Cassandra Wilson, Charles Aznavour, Charles Lloyd, Charlie Hunter (2), Cheap Trick, Chick Correa, China Moses, Christian McBride, Cindi Lauper, Clark Terry, Cris Williamson, Danilo Perez (3), Darol Anger, Dave Brubeck, Dave Van Ronk, David Bromberg, Dayramir Gonzalez, Deborah Henson-Conant (2), Didi Stewart and the Amplifiers, Dionne Warwick, Doc and Merle Watson (2), Dominique Eade, Don Byron (2), Donald Byrd, Donald Vega, Dr. John (2), Drezniak, Duke Ellington, Duke Robillard Blues Band (2), Ed Perkins Trio, Eddy Grant, Eight to the Bar, Eileen Ivers, Ella Fitzgerald, Elvis Costello and the Attractions, Emerson String Quartet, Emmanual Ax, Emmylou Harris, Ethel Merman (2), Fathead Newman, Fiction Plane, Four Tops, Frankie Valley and the Four Seasons, Freddie Hubbard, Gary Burton, Gato Barbieri, Geno Delafose, George Winston (2), Gideon Kremer, Gladys Knight and the Pips (2), Gonzalo Rubalcaba, Gordon Lightfoot, Gwen Verdon, Hall & Oates,

Herbie Mann, Holly Near, Ilana Vered, Ilton Wjuniski, Isaac Stern, Isaiah Collier, Itzhak Perlman, J.B. Hutto and The Newhawks, Jackson Browne, Jaki Byard (2), James Greene, James Taylor, Jane Monheit, Janice Ian, Jazzhounds, Jean-Pierre Rampal, Jerry Jeff Walker, Jesse Colin Young, Jimmy Cliff (2), Jimmy McLean Quintet (2), Jimmy Rushing, Jimmy Smith, Joan Armatrading, Joan Baez, Joan Jett and the Blackhearts (2), John Compton, John Gibbons, John Hammond, John Lincoln Wright, John Renbourn, John Steele Ritter, Jon Hendricks, Jonathan Edwards, Joseph Silverstein, Josephine Baker, Joshua Redman (2), Judy Collins, Jules Shear, Julliard String Quartet, Kal, Kate, Alex, and Hugh Taylor and Skin Tight, Keith Jarrett, Kendrick Oliver and The New Life Orchestra, Kim Kashkashian, La Peste, Ladysmith Black Mumbazo (2), Larry Goldings, Laurie Anderson, Lee Dorsey, Leon Parker, Leonard Cohen, Lightning Express, Linda May Han Oh, Lip, Los Lobos, Louden Wainwright, Louis Armstrong, Luisa Maita, Luther "Guitar Junior" Johnson, Manuel Gonzalez, Mark Murphy, Mars Volta, Martha and The Vandellas, Mary Black, Maynard Ferguson, Memphis Slim, Men Without Hats, Mendelbaum, Merle Haggard (2), Michael Williams, Midnight Traveler, Mikis Theodorakis, Mimi Jones, Mose Allison (3), Mott The Hoople, Natalie MacMaster (2), Newbury Chamber Music Group, Nick Lowe, Nina Simone, Noah Preminger, Oliver Mtukudzi, Orpheus, Oscar Peterson, Pastiche (3), Pat Matheny (2), Patricia Kopatchinskaja, Patricia Zander, Patty Larkin, Paul Rishell, Paul Simon, Peter Tosh (2), Phoebe Snow (2), Planet Street, Poncho Sanchez (2), Prince, Psychedelic Furs, Rancid, Ravi (2) and Anouska Shankar, Ray Charles (2), Redwing, Regina Carter (2), Renee Rosnes, Richard Thompson, Ricky Nelson, Robert Dick, Robert Palmer, Robert Stallman, Robert Taub, Roberta Flack, Robin Lane and The Chartbusters, Rodriguez, Ron Carter (4), Ronnie Gilbert, Roomful of Blues, Roxy Music, Rudolf Serkin (2), Russell Malone, Ruth Brown, Sam & Dave, Sam Jones, Sandra Wright, Sass, Segovia, Shadowfax, Sheila E.,

Sleepy LaBeef (2), Someone and The Somebodies, Sonny Rollins (2), Sonny Saul, Sonny Stitt, Soulive, Spider John Koerner, Squeeze, Stan Strickland, Stefan Harris & Blackheart, Stevie Wonder, Stories, Suzanne Vega, System of a Down, T.S. Monk (2), Taj Mahal, Talking Heads (4), Tania Maria, Taxi Boys, The Alarm, The Allman Brothers, The Atlantics, The B Girls, The Black Eyed Peas, The Blind Boys of Alabama, The Blues Project, The Cars, The Clash (2), The Cowboy Junkies, The Dark, The English Beat, The Eurythmics, The Fools, The Four Tops, The Go Gos, The John Coster Band (3), The Joy of Cooking, The Kinks, The Motels, The New Models, The New Orleans Jazz Orchestra, The Pencils, The Platters (2), The Police, The Preservation Hall Band (3), The Pretenders (2), The Raconteurs, The Ramones, The Rolling Stones (2), The Runes, The Sandra Wright Blues Band, The Stompers, The Temptations, The Who (3), The Women of the Calabash, Thelonious Monk (3), Thrills, Tim Hardin, Tom Petty, Tom Rush (2), U2, UB40, Van Morrison, Vanilla Fudge, Vince Guaraldi, Vladimir Ashkenazy, Vladimir Horowitz, Waverly Consort, Wes Montgomery (2), Will Ackerman, Woody Allen, Wynton Kelly, Yamato, Yo Yo Ma (2), Zoot Sims (2), and others not recalled: jazz, classical and rock...

**Spring Fever #2**

It's here now: I'm acting crazy
and blaming it on the weather.
Feeling fine, comfortable, gleeful
near a growing vine; birds have be-
gun to return in substantial numbers

and strut their stuff as if they owned
the joint once again. All seems delirious.
Robins are bobbing about for worms to eat.
Ants are absolutely everywhere. Greens have
become extraordinary and enormous. It's more

than temperatures rising-- humans are out in full
force, smiling at one another, grinning at nothing in
particular. Warmth has sprung; possibility is present.
We shed layers of clothing, recalling what it's all about,
given one more chance, another springtime to celebrate.

## Still Life #8

Good to go.
Senatorial
material.
Talking
smack.

Tales
of woe.
Crossing
my heart
& hoping

I don't die
today, or
ever, actually.
Fooling myself.
Running for office.

Business as usual,
with a brisk breeze
sweet-talking me now.
A freak show of a kind.
Instincts got me this far,

and I anticipate going on
until I cannot any longer.
Some say I am deft, some
daft & I think the world of
them, needing their votes.

**Stoking the Fire**

I found myself at last.
It was about time. If I

had gone any longer
I might've lost sight

of what I was so good at.
A jam session put a smile

on my face as I played my
tin sandwich. Others were

as elated. That is how it goes on
occasion. Our night was unusual.

My fate has always been entangled
with the music I so love to listen to.

**Strings Attached**

He knows deep inside
he is merely a puppet.

## The Fans Went Wild

The fans went nuts. The home town team put on quite a show. Even even-keeled people lost it and screamed. There was a full moon above Fenway as the World Series brought excitement to every single corner.

Millions watched in bars & homes, and such shouting was all rolled into one. Something was happening, then something wasn't happening. Much was at stake. Batter up & strike him out & knock one in & yea & hurray.

**Titles I Have Known**

If the Skin Fits, Wear It.

Aboveboard Half the Time.

Honk If You Give Two Shits.

What in the Name of God?

Beats the Stuffing Out of Me.

I Don't Believe the Half of It.

I've a Magnus Opus in Me.

I've Never Had the Pleasure.

Not on My Watch You Don't.

Wet Blankets Need Not Apply.

We All Have Something to Hide.

I Pay Everyone Under the Table.

Hot Shots Bite the Dust as Well.

Cool Cats Have A Chance to Win.

Make Me Feel Like a Billion Bucks.

**To-Do**

My to-do list gets longer and longer.
All that leg-work must be done by
sundown. Hold on to your hat. I
must drive my tractor over to
Payack's for a tune-up. Must
buy Bradford a birthday gift,
because a little birdie told
me he is turning seventy
on Friday. I think I know
what I'll get him. He is in
love with a kind of gismo.
I must bone-up on Alaska,
as I'll be going there next
week, and must pick out
books to take with me. I
already know I'll take a
story collection by one
of the best: Flannery
O'Connor. I must call
my dentist about a
troublesome tooth.
I must not lose my
bearings whatso-
ever. Go trim my
sideburns. Take
one more look
in the mirror,
just because I
might want to.
No not hardly.

**True Love**

      For Puddin'

Furry.
Feisty.
Feline.

Faithful
friends
forever.

## Universe Verse

Flying saucers
seek cups
for high tea.

I'm always on
the lookout
for aliens with

great answers to our
every question-- they
might have solutions,

yet the military would
most probably shoot
them down before we

had a chance to find
anything out. That is
their way. Shoot first

and sigh later.
Please pass
the pills.

**Viceroy of Variety**

I take my oeuvre over-easy.
Honest as I am, a purist at
times, at times not, I told a
friend named Peter he was
all wet, and he told me it was
the funniest thing I had ever
said. He's mad about weather.

I write about everything, as I
believe it's all of equal value.
White lies are up there with
point people, loosy goosies,
wrath, long hauls, & shoulders
to cry on. That is what I must do.
I gather my thoughts, then write.

## Walden Pond

How can this glorious day,
here, where Thoreau once

lived, not make us wistful,
as we rest on a boulder by

the water's edge? It is now.
Remember it forever or die

trying. What else is there?
Yet our lot insists-- we go.

It tries my patience, my
having to be elsewhere.

These good old days are here,
true enough, and in no time

we are gone, because it seems
we need to be somewhere else.

Nameless is what we are.
Not the opposite. I am at

a loss. My inner life is filled
full of the names of absents.

**Why Was I Born?**

To listen to jazz, certainly.
To look at and collect art.

To adore two offspring.
To publish many books.

To write tons of poems
and dream my dreams...

Love Lori a lot. Make
sense of things. Laugh.

Remember and honor my
mother who I never knew.

Be generous to others; to make
my friends happier than before.

To root the Boston Red Sox on
as hard as conceivably possible.

Read, write, buy books,
and witness my times. I

am aware of all of that,
but what am I missing?

It is anyone's guess.
That says something.

I will spend the rest of my days
searching for what I don't know.

## Wishful Thinking #2

Brattle Birds
read books be-
fore breakfast.

They prize
rhyme at
the right time

living in the
poetry nearby.
Appreciate them

today, before they
soar far, far, far away.
Some birds rise higher

than others. Some fly true,
working hard to stay aloft.
Never underestimate them.

**Wishing**

    A Prayer in Memory of John Lennon (12/80)

I wish women had the same rights as men.
That blacks had the same rights as whites.

That guns were outlawed, war impossible,
that the starving had food, that the sad

were glad, that the air & water was clean.
That everyone was free, as free as can be.

**You Ask Stupid Questions**
**You Get Stupid Answers**

Why did you get into boxing
in the first place, and couldn't
you think of something more
important to do? Isn't boxing
destructive, awfully violent?

I got into boxing to beat the crap
out of people. I'm a violent person
with a need to cause bodily harm.
Now if you will move out of my way
I've got to go and smash something.

**Yours Truly**

Such a nag. I am always after myself to get it correct, to get it done, finish up what I've started and then some, but I am the first one to pat myself on the back as well. I notice what others don't see, and I am okay with that. The world does not revolve around me, and that's a good thing. I love my peace and quiet.

**Roland Pease** founded Zoland Books in Cambridge, Massachusetts with his wife, Lori. He was the editor there for fifteen years before becoming the fiction and poetry editor at Steerforth Press, in Hanover, New Hampshire. He was also an editor at Phone-A-Poem, and at *Zoland Poetry, an Annual of Poems, Translations and Interviews*. He has had poems published in *The Paris Review, The Boston Globe, The New York Times, Let the Bucket Down, Can We Have Our Ball Back,* and other publications.

www.ingramcontent.com/pod-product-compliance
Lightning Source LLC
Chambersburg PA
CBHW051700040426
42446CB00009B/1229